WELCOME TO THE BIKE FACTORY

WELCOME TO THE BIKE FACTORY

DERRICK BUTTRESS

All rights reserved. No part of this work covered by the copyright hereon may be reproduced or used in any means – graphic, electronic, or mechanical, including copying, recording, taping, or information storage and retrieval systems – without written permission of the publisher.

Printed by imprintdigital
Upton Pyne, Exeter
www.imprintdigital.net

Typeset by narrator
www.narrator.me.uk
info@narrator.me.uk

Published by Shoestring Press
19 Devonshire Avenue, Beeston, Nottingham, NG9 1BS
(0115) 925 1827
www.shoestringpress.co.uk

First published 2014
© Copyright: Derrick Buttress

The moral right of the author has been asserted.

ISBN 978 1 910323 00 7

ACKNOWLEDGEMENTS

Acknowledgements are due to the following magazines in which some of these poems, or versions of them, first appeared: *Brittle Star*; *The Frogmore Papers*; *The Interpreter's House*; *Links*; *The New Writer*; *Other Poetry*; *Penniless Press*; *Poetry Nottingham*; *Smiths Knoll*; *South*; *Staple*.

'Running Boy', 'Girl Power' and 'The Mason on York Minster' first appeared in *Spiking the Boss's Gin*, Mosaic, 1998. 'The Village' won first prize in the Nottingham Evening Post competition. 'Welcome to the Bike Factory'; appeared in the anthology *Work* published by Katabasis, 1999.

For Joan, Kathryn and Rachel

CONTENTS

First Fire	1
The Ice House	2
The Bard for Boys	3
Running Boy	4
Photograph of a Sailor	5
Eric	6
Bookworm	8
Country Boy	9
How to Steal Apples	10
Footloose	12
The Village, 1950	14
On Our Street	16
Welcome To The Bike Factory	17
The Scent of Oranges	18
Sleeving	20
Girl Power	21
Working Girls	22
Radford Pit	24
A Stockinger's Life, 1841	25
The Mason on York Minster	26
Dante Alighieri Sees Beatrice	27
The Iron Age	28
Genesis	29
The Vanishing Isle	30
New Car on the Estate	32
The Past	33
Space	34
Looking for Charlie	35
After the Accident	36
Verb	37

FIRST FIRE

A frail wisp of smoke rises
from stubborn coals.
There is no flame, no heat.
She kneels on rough, bare boards,
patient as a supplicant,
coaxes a struggling fire
to warm an empty house.

She struggles with the baffling fireplace,
a mad contraption of doors and levers
in black enameled iron.
A mystery until now, it leaps into life
with a sudden roar, offers its first flame.

She laughs, rocks the damper
until a violent draught sucks in smoke,
swallows it deep into a chamber
hidden from sight in the chimney back.
Flames leap up, blue and yellow flowers
of welcome blossoming among the coals.
They warm this new house, make it home.

THE ICE HOUSE

We found it in a corner of the field
beyond the orchard that we scrumped,
a mound of grass, like a giant grave,
full of a darkness that was tangible ,
that we might stroke like a pelt
if we dared to reach in and touch.
It stank like a dead dog in a ditch.

We were sure it was the pit
where bad dreams hid until dark,
creeping out stinking of old shirts and armpits,
the den of a nightmare creature
that knew our names and where we lived,
the home of a ghost that would crawl
into our restless sleep at night.
Stoning it from a distance, we took pot-shots
at the unknown through a hanging door,
listening for an echo to gauge its depth.

What was that sound we heard?
The scuttle of rats mad with hunger searching
through bones of the estate's lost cats?
Or was it all our demons leaping out to chase us?
It's what we told the girls to make them scream,
and half believed ourselves, racing home
before evening claimed the fading summer light.

THE BARD FOR BOYS

After the gym display we perform
a crippled Midsummer Night's Dream.
The spotlight falls on artisans and fairies,
cardboard spectacle and belly-laughs.
Puck the sprite is Ken, the school's high jumper,
Oberon, the King of Fairyland
is Baz, ace on a rope.
Titania, Queen of the fairies is Tim.
who can still sing soprano.

I'm a mumbling Quince, leading a gang
of artisans dumb with stage-fright.
We were not chosen for our thespian gifts,
but because we could read,
Bottom the weaver is Ginger George,
tug-of war anchorman,
the fattest lad in the year,
that being considered comic enough.

Mincing Mr Vine loans his record
of Mendelssohn's creepy incidental music.
It gives our show its only touch of class,
echoing art drowning out the clatter
of a slum boys' Shakespearian shambles.

What was it all about? Mam asks.
I'm not sure, I say as we walk home.
Something to do with ignorant peasants
putting on a play, I think.
It was long, Mam says. Very long.

RUNNING BOY

Smith had a bony skull
and a smile like winter.
Flagpole thin, his clothes
flapped in the breeze.

When the cold wind
blew from the fields
his narrow chest rattled
like a dry machine.

A born victim, his cries
made mongrels bolt,
neighbours start in wonder
as from a holy curse.

The mother, a hymn loving
hater of boys, dark and mean,
with a face like a funeral in the rain,
had a soul of iron.

She made him run errands
for his keep, a skinny boy sprint
there and back in double quick time,
past our idle play, our contempt,

piston legs carrying him
beyond our horizons,
beyond the child in him,
our mockery yelping at his heels.

PHOTOGRAPH OF A SAILOR

The boy is home on leave,
and leary in his uniform.
He sticks his photograph
on the bedroom wall,
beside his pose in boxing gear.
Soon he'll be sent to sea.

Sleepless on a destroyer riding
winter storms in the Atlantic
in darkness and through ice,
he hears a torpedo's punch,
the shudder of a dying vessel.
HMS *Windsor* cracks open like a nut.

Leaping into an oil-slicked sea,
he hears shipmates shout,
cry out for their mothers,
grow quiet, then drift away.

Back home he is a stranger now,
his larking soured by curt aggression.
The boy has become a man,
locked in a room of bitterness
until those that love him find the key.

ERIC

He didn't look right,
he was all loose legs and flapping hands,
all bony knees and elbows.
Half-starved and pasty faced,
his ears turned livid pink in frosty weather.
He was the kid who got slapped on the head
in the playground for being puny.
A kid who shivered a lot,
stuffing his hands up the sleeves
of his woolly jumper,
(the one with snot-stiffened cuffs.)
He was so bedraggled on the way to school
we thought he'd been left out all night.
We suffered him, because his dad was dead.
We knew God was looking,
so treated him right, believing kids
with dead dads were different, specially chosen.
Seeing a dead dad's face made them different.
They knew something we didn't:
it was the secret our parents whispered
about at the funerals
of dead grandmas and grandads.
He knew what a dead man looked like
and that was his secret,
the one we daren't broach.
And his mam was strange, too.
She stood on her step watching him
play with us, shouting after him;
'Don't go off the street!
Come in when it gets dark!'

So we let this half-orphan walk with us,
forgave him his half-barmy mam,
his snotty sleeves and his total failure
to jump a fence, or climb a tree,
without falling arse-over-tip on his face.
After all, his dad was dead.

BOOKWORM

Barred from the streets
by endless days of illness,
he despised his narrow room.
Too breathless for the world,
he created a version of his own
behind a barricade of pulp.
Each book helps his heart beat
faster, makes him strong.

Through sleepless nights
he reads stories of hard-nosed cops,
mono emotional in six-word vocabularies,
chain smokers who stalked the city
comforted by icy blondes,
embraced for a meaningless hour.

He dreamed he was a private-eye,
One who walked alone,
making the world equal
with a gat, his only friend,
surviving by the skin of his teeth
and learning to live with lonliness.

COUNTRY BOY

Sent to a school for dunces,
his skill was in silent trespass.
He learned to raid the big-house gardens,
skimmed stones and broken slates
across the quarry's dangerous pool,
its still, black water deep enough to drown a boy.
Laughing, he ran from farmer's dogs
and keepers swearing as they chased.

Scrumping early-season fruit,
he loved the taste of bitter apples,
pears with flesh hard as conkers.
He loved the private woods, the fear in them,
listened to the Spring song of the blackbird,
the wren, the robin and the thrush.
His fingers, scratched and bleeding,
lifted warm eggs from nests he marvelled at.

Walking the country miles
through summer rain,
laughing at his drenching,
he learned to read the fields and woods
which told a story he could understand.

HOW TO STEAL APPLES

Ignore the stone-pocked *Private* signs
as you walk through farms and fields.
Skirt the acres of ripening wheat,
crawl through gaps in hawthorn and wire,
a trespasser, scratched and grazed.

Climb the low hill to enter a copse
made dark by rhododendrons grown rank.
Deep inside the wood break back
tangled branches and twigs,
force a path to the squawk and scuffle
of birds whose nests you seek.

By the ancient pool, lie on your stomach
to search its muddy bed for the fabulous carp
no-one has ever hooked.
Be wary of the swan with the evil eye
and the hiss of a snake!
Its thrashing wings would break an arm.
In the water's coal-black mirror
watch rooks circle on the rising air.

It is time, now, to raid the orchard,
time to fill your shirt with sour, green apples
that tastes of wood so bitter
it bites the tongue, brings on a belly-ache.
Now turn for home, crossing baking summer fields.
Suck a stalk of grass for its sweet juice
as you squint at the dazzling sky.

Hawthorn hedges, the *Private* signs
and wire fences that slash and cut
should never keep you from the orchard.
The landscape that you roam is truly yours.
The hard green apples that you scrump
belong to you by right of being bold enough
to pluck them off the rich man's tree.

FOOTLOOSE

We're messing about on the road
trying to think of something to do
in the middle of a dead Sunday,
so we welcome the interruption
when this big bloke with tattoos
of zigzag lightning on his neck lurches up.

He asks if he's on the right road for Glasgow:
How do I get to fucking Glasgow?
We want to laugh because Scotland
is just a rumour this far south,
and our road leads nowhere much.
But we don't because we're daren't.
His shoulders are as broad as a barn door,
and his clenched fists look like a threat.
One punch would flatten my nose.

He asks us if we've got any dosh
for something to eat, because he's hungry.
We don't like to think what might happen
if we refuse, so we hand over a couple of quid
we manage to scrape together.
He gives a sort of grunt, and gobs
before he swings around,
lurching back the way he came.

When he's gone, we talk
about how we might walk away one day:
be kind of loose and free and dangerous,
frightening the shit out of people.
It would be better than wasting time
waiting for life to start.

All you can do in a dump like ours
is count the days until
it's time to do a runner.
Maybe to *fucking Glasgow*. Or anywhere.

THE VILLAGE, 1950

That summer kids ran wild
through lush pastures, and the woods,
chased rabbits in fields of ripening wheat.

The youngest found mischief by the brook,
filled jam jars with fish like tiny points of light,
hunted frogs under slimy banks, teased neurotic coots.

All learned to nest the hawthorn hedge,
probe the secret life of birds
with bleeding fingers, stole their eggs.

In orchards strictly out of bounds
the bravest climbed ancient apple trees,
hurled half-grown fruit at passing rooks.

At summer's end, more than a season passed.
The children watched roots of oak and elm
torn out, nests crushed beneath steel tracks,

rooks float on air, searching for their roost
as machines gouged out roads
through stubble, warm still in the sun.

Couples from the stifling streets of town
moved out, at last, of the shadow of war,
the slow moving years of loss and separation.

They turned new-cut keys in locks
of houses that smelled of wood, fresh paint,
heard rooms settling as though they were alive.

In gardens cut out of pasture they sowed seeds,
saw needle-fine tips of grass grow lush,
wondered at the flowers they couldn't name.

ON OUR STREET

Baz is in a battle of wills
with his Staffy bitch, a delinquent
pulling hard against an elastic lead.
By his side, slagging each other off,
his children, the turbulent twins:
Kira and Kevin in espressivo mode,
the cause of their kick-box altercation
deeply lost in adolescent pidginise.

Baz would rather be alone.
Kevin wants to punch something..
Kira is looking for a laugh.
Their mam, back home, is marooned
far off on a fag and tablet island.
Baz hauls in the bitch,
yells at the twins as they reach the mall.
He would die for one day that was different.

WELCOME TO THE BIKE FACTORY

We will begin with the history of the Company,
how six artisans of the old school
sweated over the manipulation of steel
until even their skill could not keep pace,
how the genius with an eye on the future
broke down the art into function,
the skill into units of wealth
that paid ten thousand numbers
clocking on, clocking off

followed by advice

on how not to get crushed, cut or torn,
what to do if you find a finger missing,
(what to do with the missing finger)
how to deal with shock, electrocution,
broken foot bones and skin disease
(through no fault of ours)
what to say to the man with the tang
of a file thrust \through his wrist
and other information
relevant to your survival:

your point of departure
your chance of promotion
what we will pay you
what it will cost you

after which we will convey you
to the assembly line
to the assembly line
to the assembly line

THE SCENT OF ORANGES

Palestine smelled of oranges.
He remembered that for fifty years
after he was shipped to London for work
in his brother's Whitechapel sweatshop.
There he met the Jewish tailors of Poland.
They knew the meaning of work.
He believed the Rabbi when he told him
the history of the Jews
was a history of hard labour.

Having a brother as a boss
was no comfort to a young Jew
on a sewing machine.
The boy worked twelve hours a day,
and longer when work was urgent.
He machined overcoat linings
until he was dizzy with fatigue.
Sometimes, his brother made him work
by candlelight to save money on the electric,
rapping his knuckles with a brass-edged rule
when the ache in his fingers sent the seam awry.

He told me that if I had worked in such days
it would have made a man of me.
I told him I was man enough, thank you,
and praised God Almighty
for the Garment Workers Union.

He tried to work even when cancer wrecked him.
He struggled to the factory one day
and collapsed over his Singer sewing machine.
He had sewed his last seam.
I didn't like him much, but I remember him,
sometimes, if I catch the scent of oranges.

SLEEVING

The fullness of the cloth must fall
into the hollow of the scye
to form a perfect drape.
Seam an even width,
the sewing a constant
measured by the experience of the eye.
Ease in the fabric smoothly
and at speed
matching stripe to stripe
on a patterned cloth,
notch to notch,
feeding cloth to the needle
with firm fingers, a kind of sweep
of the practised hand
until seam meets seam
to complete the act
and the sleeve is set.
Then do it all again, and again,
a hundred times a day
while the hard, white light
burns away each crawling hour.

GIRL POWER

The smart girls
of our town swing
in their little black suits
and their little black shoes
go *clickity-clack*
on the pavements
before the shining towers
of commerce.

Their eyes are bright
as marble, their colours
warmed by the jitters.
The black cases they clutch
bulge with ambition
and a little light lunch.

I have nothing to do
but to love them
as they rush to work,
light as dancers,
away from me
like daughters
leaving home.

WORKING GIRLS

> Contained in Reports of the Sadler Committee and the Ashley Miner's Commission in Parliamentary Papers, 1831-32 and 1842.

Elizabeth Bentley aged 23
I was six years old when I started
at Mr Busk's mill as a little doffer.
We worked from 5 in the morning till 9 at night
when they was thronged.
When we flagged they would strap us severely.
I was always on time, for my mother
had been up at three o'clock in the morning
when she heard the colliers going to their work.
I have sometimes walked to the mill
at four o'clock in the morning,
and waited outside
when it was streaming down with rain.

Sarah Gooder aged 8
I'm a trapper in the Gawber pit.
It does not tire me,
but I have to trap without a light
and I'm scared.
I go at half-past three in the morning
and come out at half-past five in the afternoon.

Sometimes I sing when it is light,
but not in the dark.
I dare not sing then.
I go to school on Sunday
and learn *Reading Made Easy*.
They teach me to pray:
God bless me and make me a good servant.

Patience Kershaw aged 17
I go to the pit at five o'clock
and come out at five in the evening.
I hurry the corves a mile or more underground,
and wear a belt and chains.
The getters beat me with their hands
on my back if I am not quick.
Sometimes they pull me about.
There are 20 boys and 15 men,
and all the men are naked.
I am the only girl.

RADFORD PIT

Gill and Carson
Randell and Fewkes
Black water seeps into their footprints,
the toxic air gathers up their echoes.
Their sweat is the rime on a post
rooted in the past.

Walker and Jones
Bostock and Varley
Blue scars never fade
on the skin of old men
spitting into a cold wind.

Browitt and Starr
Francis and Buck
Iron and coal shaped them,
water and stone destroyed them
their history buried beneath the dust.

A STOCKINGER'S LIFE, 1841

That of John Radford,
born by the Bull Well
as a burden on the Parish,
by whose charitable hand
he was given strict measure
of governance and raised up
on bread and cold porridge.

He was cared for by those
who loved God and all His creation,
but found the orphan hard to take,
taught to know his place
in the scheme of things temporal,
which was lowly among men,
but high in the workhouse roof
where the pigeons crooned to him,
and the rain sang him to sleep.

Later, he lived in Cabbage Alley,
sharing three rooms in a back-to -back
with a skinny wife who expected
no more than the poverty she got.
Each morning he woke to hear
the knocker's rap on the window,
survived the cholera years,
watched his children grow,
taught himself to read and write.

THE MASON ON YORK MINSTER

Climbing from earth to sky
he shapes the stones
against the inconstant years.
He speaks only with his hands
of what comes after the pangs
of the century's hunger,
the failures of the heart.

From apprentice to master
it is here in the raising of the stone
he comes to know himself, at last,
against the fickle seasons,
the dust in the throat.

It is here, spitting into the wind,
he feels the long winter in his bones,
trusts in his mastery of space,
carves in light the imago of his faith
on the cold, clear summit of the north.

DANTE ALIGHIERI SEES BEATRICE

The first letter of each word spells out the name.

Devil's advocates, nubile tarts entice,
affecting love,
Italy's godless hookers
imbibing every ratsbane imaginable:
double applejacks, nog,
tequila, even absinthe.

Later, immaculate girls
(haughtily indifferent)
emerge, reigniting instantly
Dante's ardour.

Now the exquisite angel,
looking ineffably graceful,
heaven's innocent,
enters regally.
Idyllic days are nigh.

Temptation ensnares all lovers;
inamoratas gladden hearts inordinately.
Especially raunchy Italians.

THE IRON AGE

Lying in the grave we dug
he looked too humble an offering.
We wondered if he was up to the job
we'd planted him for, if we'd fail again,
spend another season hungry.

We chanted the old plea in a cloud
of moths drawn by our torches,
begged the gods to forgive us
our bad luck, our frail resolve,
then offered up a sacrifice of corn
meant for our children's bellies.
Finally, we buried the tools honed
for a harvest the earth denied us.

Next morning we wandered back
after a restless night of rain.
The grave was empty.
The wind scattered sodden ears of corn.
Somebody said *wolves,* somebody swore,
spat six feet into a freezing wind.
We returned across cold fields,
hunger rooted in our guts,
the wolves circling the horizon.

GENESIS

In the beginning there was Toad,
God's gift to planet earth.
Composed of mud and primal rain
a billion years have kept him pure.

Toad's chrysoberyl eye blinks
once in every season.
A clock ticks inside his brain.

In autumn he tunnels
in rain-softened earth
to hunker under winter frost.

There he waits for spring,
the procreative urge that sends him
in search of sex, wearing the face
of a penitent at Lent.

THE VANISHING ISLE

> About these parts are certain flitting Isles
> and when men look upon them they vanish.
> – John Sparke, 1564

Atlantic waters swell like molten glass
moved by the power of the tide.
Only a swallow may break the surface
when it rises from its nest beneath the waves.

From a distance sailors stare
at crystal mountains lost in icy clouds,
sail on to find a beach of hot, white sand
many leagues in length,
beguiling voyagers to Paradise.

But when a ship draws near St Brendan's Isle
it becomes most strangely shy,
for it vanishes at once,
sinking beneath the waters
like a leaking skiff.

Below the deck
of a creaking barque
the crew of scratching jacks,
asleep on gently swaying beds,
dream of England, its women and its ale.

They care little
for this oceanic sleight of hand,
know only that the isle
becomes a phantom when approached
by gents with bibles in their satchels,
an eye for gold
and the sweat of avarice
staining their fine-stitched brocatelle.

NEW CAR ON THE ESTATE

Then one morning
a brand new Ford appeared
parked on a road down which
only milk floats and bread vans ventured.
Pausing on our way to work
at the bike factory, we circled it
in dumb wonder, awestruck
by the glossy black paint job.
It promised money to burn,
luxury, the first sign of affluence
after the small-change years.

Here before us was the promised future,
built like a cheap tin toy
with three useless dials
set in its flimsy dashboard,
wind-up, wind-down windows,
and padded seats so thin
they would make your bones ache
before you reached the end of the road.
We bent down to sniff its exciting aroma:
the stink of rubber, the whiff of petrol,
searched for a flash of chrome, found none,
but admired the streamline of boot and bonnet.

The car was definitely a sign
of the good times coming our way,
the end of mean living,
the demise of scrimp and scrape,
the promise of a lifetime's cushy ride
all the way to Easy Street.

THE PAST

(For J.)

The old are always living in the past,
remembering moments in a long life
as though they held a secret,
made sense of a journey they had
undertaken blindly, trusting to luck.

We thought their stories laughable,
as pointless as an outworn myth
they clung to like a fading dream,
their lives a box of forgotten letters
full of trivia, discovered in the attic
and read with tired eyes

Now I return to my own past.
In that story I make my way back
to a house illuminated by the love
of the people living there,
the laughter of children
playing in the garden.

I want to make my way to that house,
see you walk into the light
of the hall once again, smiling,
and about to utter the words
which begin a marvellous story.

SPACE

The universe is mostly empty space,
its infinity hard to visualize
fenced in, as we are, by horizons.

There are many intricate maps of space,
and beautiful photographs of galaxies
that are mysterious and far out of reach.

In the scale of things we are small,
we are very small, and the idea
of endless space makes us feel smaller.

Trying to read the universe
is like being lost in the woods, in a fog,
at midnight, as we search for a signpost.

Something we don't know about engendered
stardust, made us, will unmake us,
which, even then, might not be the end.

LOOKING FOR CHARLIE

I wander through aisles of fiction
searching for a novel that haunts me,
the title of which has swum through a hole
in my memory, like a fish out of a net.
I remember the heroine
was the kind of girl I dreamt of meeting,
though I can't recall her name.
Charlie is the only name I remember.

But that wasn't her name, of course,
and it wasn't her husband's.
He was a swine, naturally,
an expressive drunk, and unfaithful to boot,
the usual inadequate, one who drove her mad
then drove her out in despair.

Lately, the names of everyone I know
are swimming out of sight,
But I remember this novel's angry chapters,
people crying, and the Ibsenic drama of the woman
finally slamming the door on her life,
taking Charlie with her.

I've read a hundred blurbs of a hundred novels
in these endless library aisles.
They promise hours of a distant,
but exquisite pain, something like life,
a difficult journey through sex, love and death,
But none mention a dog called Charlie.

AFTER THE ACCIDENT

It was months before I resumed
my lessons in ballroom dancing.
I managed a limping waltz
executed a fox-trot, after a fashion,
but the quick-step was impossible.
The only dance my crippled style
suited was the Argentine tango.
Strangers assumed I had been wounded
in one of the recent wars.
The truth was, I had fallen off my bike.
In cold weather I slid through snow
as though I was wearing skis.

Not until I discovered that Byron,
our local literary nob, had stomped
around the town on a club foot boot
did I realize the kudos
that lay in a charismatic limp.

I tried my hand at poetry,
dreamed that my limp was a sign
of the creative spirit, a gift from my muse,
evidence of something romantically tragic about me.
My limp made me a poet.
It gave me an affinity with Lord Byron,
although I hadn't read any of his poems.

I regretted my ignorance of everything
but the relentless, workaday grind,
the twisted knot of my tongue.
But, as a sweated labourer in a bicycle factory,
what time did I have for cultural activities,
apart from learning to dance?

VERB

Verb is a go-getter, in at everything,
wanting to do this, wanting to do that,
but most of all wanting to be *the* Verb -
the Infinite One, the one they're all scared of,
the one they take their orders from.
You won't find it happy to leave the house
without its uniform and cane.

It loves to tell a good story,
especially when the bedroom curtains
are thrown back to reveal
an extravagantly red-clouded dawn
straight out of *The Odyssey*.
It makes mornings like that mean something.

Oh, it loves the thrill of starlings
doing a wild ballet over the river
as the sun goes down.
It knows how to conjure feeling
from a scene like that all right.
It's alive. Feed it, feel its pulse.